HAVE FUN COLORING

YOUNG AUTHORKDP

MON
STAR

MON

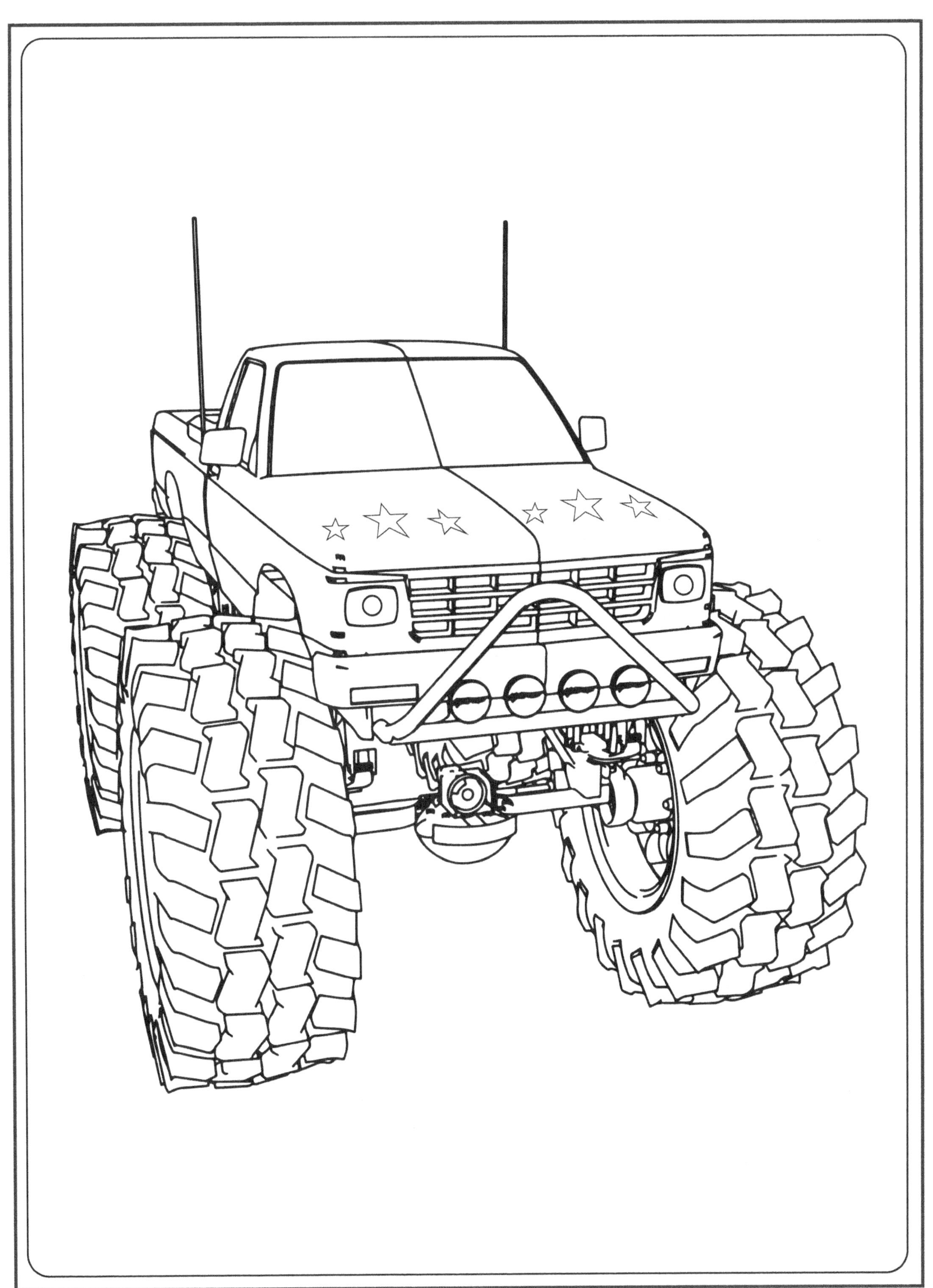

YOUNG AUTHORKDP

YOUNG AUTHORKDP

YOUNG AUTHORKDP

TRAXXAS
T-MAXX

YOUNG AUTHORKDP

YOUNG AUTHORKDP

YOUNG AUTHORKDP

YOUNG AUTHORKDP

YOUNG AUTHORKDP

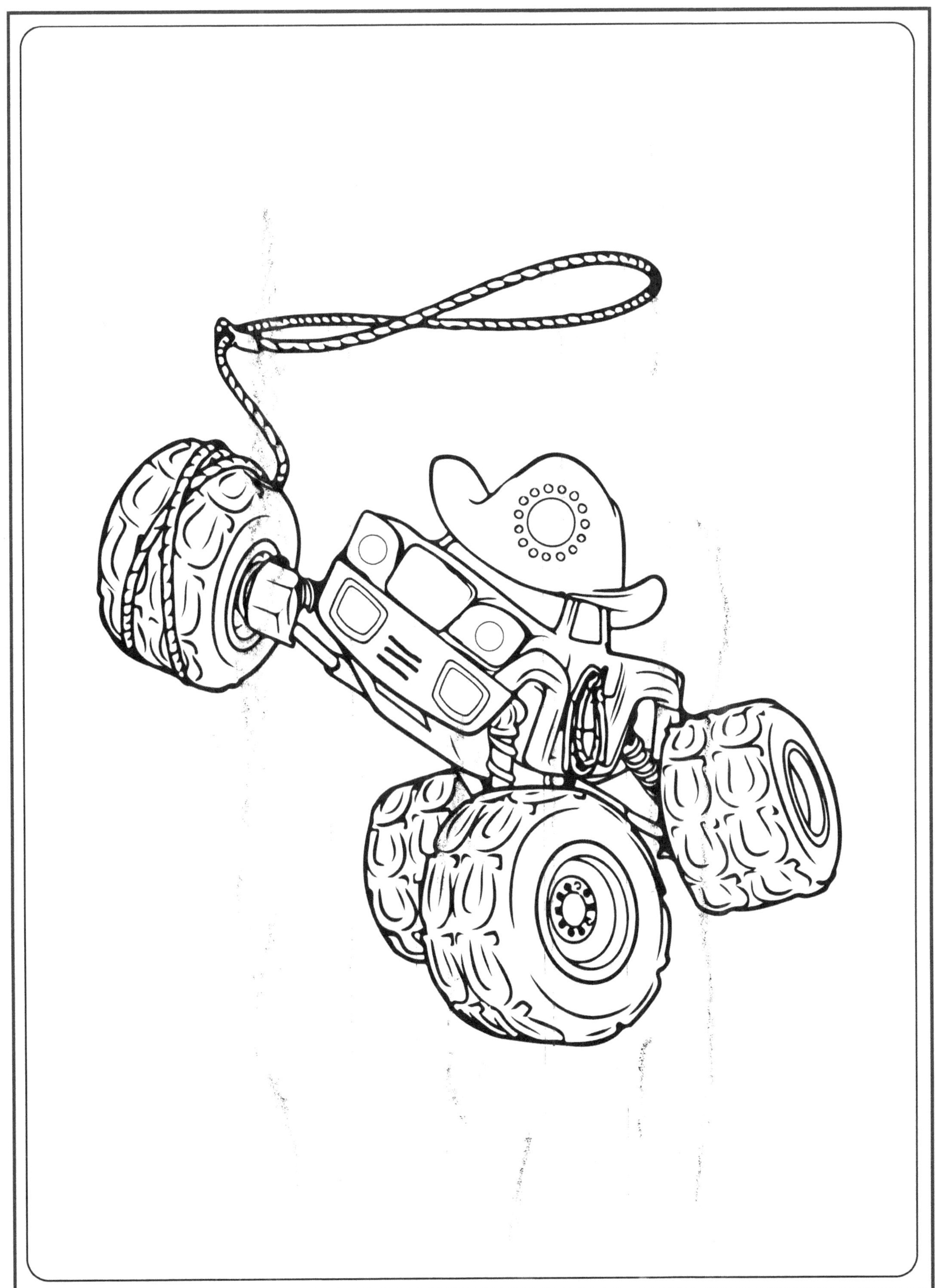

YOUNG AUTHORKDP

YOUNG AUTHORKDP

MON

YOUNG AUTHORKDP

YOUNG AUTHORKDP

YOUNG AUTHORKDP